NATIONAL GEOGRAPHIC **OUR WORLD**

Art Class

by Yuko Okamura

  NATIONAL GEOGRAPHIC LEARNING | CENGAGE Learning

"Are there more crayons?" the students ask.

"Yes, there are," says the teacher.

"What are you doing?" asks the teacher.

"We're drawing and coloring pictures for our poster!" say the students.

"Are there more scissors?" the students ask.

"Yes, there are," says the teacher.

"What are you doing now?" asks the teacher.

"We're cutting pictures for our poster!" say the students.

"Is there more glue?" the students ask.

"Yes, there is," says the teacher.

"What are you doing now?" asks the teacher.

"We're gluing the pictures on our poster!" say the students.

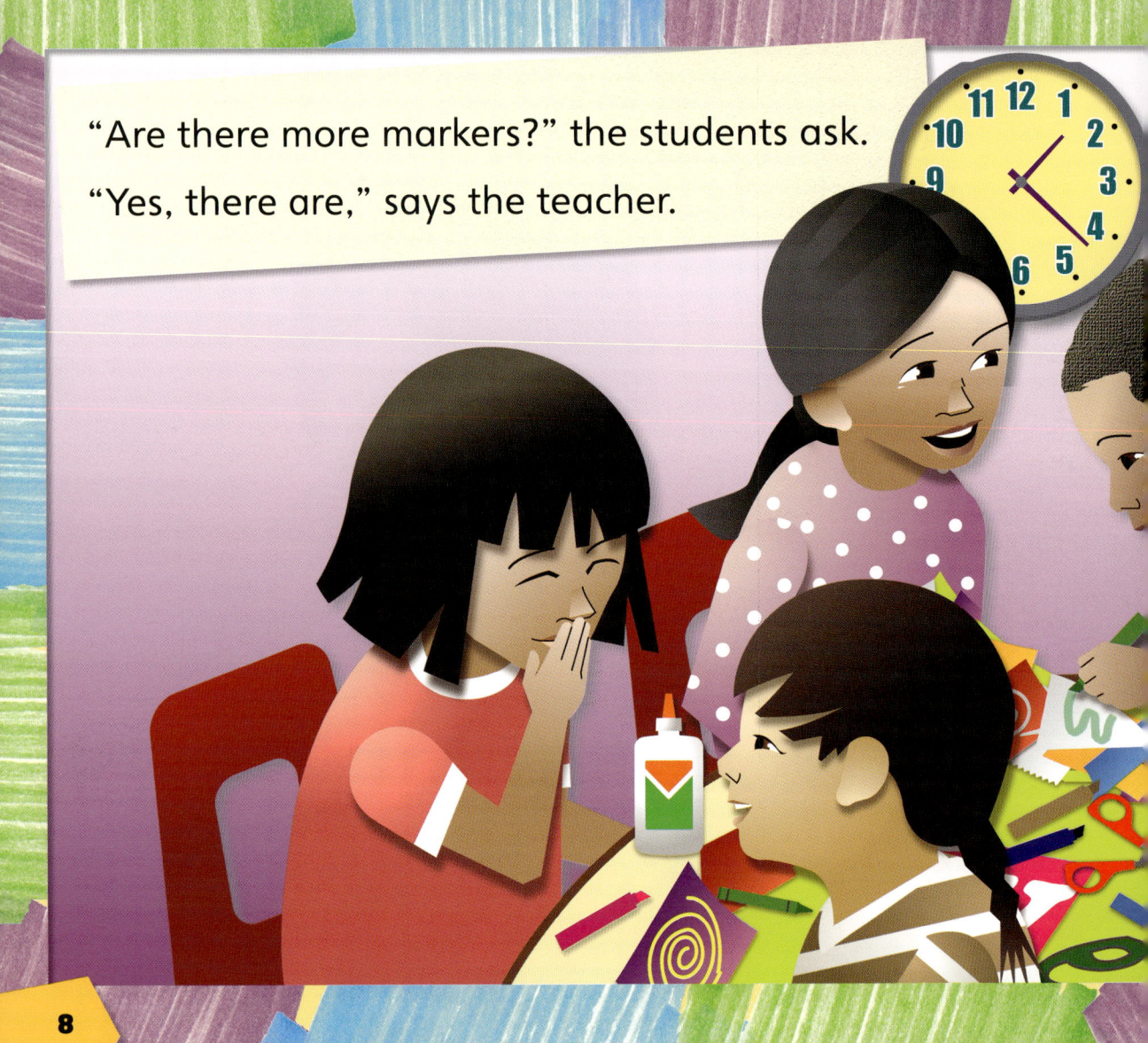

"Are there more markers?" the students ask.

"Yes, there are," says the teacher.

"What are you doing now?" asks the teacher.

"We're writing on our poster!"
say the students.

"May I see the poster?" asks the teacher.

"It's a poster about our art class,"
say the students. "We love art!"

"What a wonderful poster!"
says the teacher.

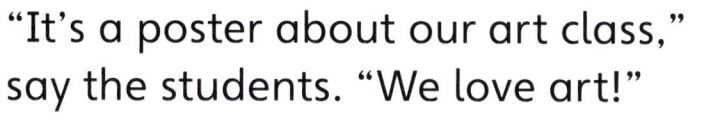

Facts About Colors

Do you like to paint? You can make painting even more fun by mixing colors.

Red, yellow, and blue are called **primary colors**. You can mix primary colors to make other colors.

red   +   yellow   =   orange

blue + **yellow** = **green**

blue + **red** = **purple**

You can make even more colors by mixing primary and non-primary colors.

red + **green** = **brown**

What other colors can you make by mixing colors?

Fun with Art

What is it? Match the words to the pictures.

scissors

glue

markers

paint

What are the students doing? Write the word.

coloring   cutting   gluing   writing

1. <u>cutting</u>

2. _____

3. _____

4. _____

Glossary

love

mix

poster